THE PSYCHIATRIST

THE PSYCHIATRIST

MARIELA GRIFFOR

NEW & SELECTED POEMS

 EYEWEAR PUBLISHING

First published in 2013
by Eyewear Publishing Ltd
74 Leith Mansions, Grantully Road
London W9 1LJ
United Kingdom

Typeset with graphic design by Edwin Smet
Author photograph Javiera Denney
Printed in England by TJ International Ltd, Padstow, Cornwall

ISBN 978-1-908998-11-8

WWW.EYEWEARPUBLISHING.COM

For
J.S. (1960-1985)
R.I.V.P. (1956-1987)
M.A.B. (1959-1991)
J.N. (1956-1987)

Mariela Griffor was born in
the city of Concepción in southern Chile.
She attended the University of Santiago and the Catholic
University of Rio de Janeiro. She left Chile for an involuntary exile
in Sweden in 1985. She and her American husband returned to the
United States in 1998 with their two daughters. They live in Grosse
Pointe Park, Michigan. She is publisher of Marick Press. Her work
has appeared in periodicals across Latin America and the United
States. Mariela holds a BA in Journalism and an MFA in Creative
Writing from New England College. She is the author of *Exiliana*
(Luna Publications) and *House* (Mayapple Press).
She is Honorary Consul of Chile in Michigan.

Table of Contents

New

There is no space wider than that of grief,
There is no universe like that which bleeds.
— Pablo Neruda

I'm an educated man, the prisons I know are subtle ones.
— Roberto Bolaño

Exiliana

Prologue I

Out here, the snow is an insider,
it's the *haute couture* of my days.
I invent a friend to pour out
remembrances of the old country.

Out here, I invent new sounds, new men, new women.
I assassinate the old days with nostalgia.
I don't see but invent a city and its people, its fury, its sky.

I don't belong to the earth but to the air.
As I invent you, I invent myself.

Love for a subversive

I

What do we do with the love if you die?
Do we put it in your coffin
together with the green, red and gray plaid shirt
you like so much?
With your khaki pants
and light brown shoes,
the ones you use in your normal life?
Or do we wrap it around
the flag the Patriotic Front militia
will bring to cover you?

I spend nights sleepless
thinking about what to do
with the love if you die.

We could put it
in a crown of flowers
like the ones people weave
for Scandinavian men
when they become bridegrooms.

Your mother would say: 'No!
Chilean men don't wear flowers on their heads.'
It would be awkward.
I understand her.

I would try to put it
in a letter that you

could read when you are alone
and lonesome.

To be honest
I don't know what to do
with the love if you die.

II

Santiago is a scarlet puddle
of idiots,
poets,
assassins, and
innocents.
You said it yourself
before it happened.

III

I remember only the
scars over your lips,
scars over your left eyebrow,
the pieces of flesh missing
around your nostrils.

The pain of your scars
wakes me up at night and I hurt
as I did giving birth to your child.

I don't know with any certainty
what to do next.

One day at a time they tell me.

I will wait until the answer
comes with clarity from
behind the smoke of the landmine
or the hand grenade that took you
away from my hand.

I will keep secret all your names,
the places where
we will raise barricades and mount
attacks on police stations
until they kill us all
or they surrender.

Sunday walk, urban talk

For Recaredo Ignacio Valenzuela

Since our conversation about Guevara failed,
nothing was going to be prolific that Sunday.
Except small disagreements.

We walked towards the gates of
O'Higgins Park, where we trained
among Santiaguinos, ice-cream parlours,
handicraft stores and armed police.

Every Sunday we entered the
park pretending to be a couple,
jogging our way away from a nightmare,
pretending you were "George" and I was "Rebecca".

In those days we didn't need much.
         A heavy ammunition was resting in our hearts.

None of us wanted to be compared with Guevara.
Too tiring. Too much. Almost a sacrilege.
Not for what people think.
None of us wanted to leave the country
or experience any adventures.

You wanted to go to your classes,
teach year after year,
come back in the evenings
and find a woman who liked you
as much as you liked her.

Myself, I wanted a garden,
big, full of plants and eccentric flowers,
to read the newspapers in the morning,
write a bit about things I couldn't say
and love "Philip" as always.

Ignacio, what happened?
We were almost sure we would make it out alive.
What kind of country is this that falls in love
with death every time freedom disappears
from its core?

What kind of country is this
that kills its own sons and daughters?

Somebody will have to wash away your blood
from Alhue Street and the river of blood on Pedro Donoso.
Someday, somebody
has to do something with it.

The Rain

The sound of the rain in Michigan
reminds me of the rugged winters in my old country:
the cold feet in old shoes,
the fast sound of the water hitting the ground,
the smell of eucalyptus in the air.
I close my eyes and make a wish:
wish I could see, for just a moment, your hair
dancing over your face
trying to escape the weather.
I wish I could see again your hands looking
for a warm, soft place as a shelter in my body.
I wish the rain would never stop.

I open my eyes and know I am here
listening without you.
The clock from the dining room tells me it
is past midnight,
the rain still plays in the garden and on
the streets of Detroit
washing away disillusionment, bad thoughts,
cleansing the sirens of the police cars,
washing little by little the fear of
new encounters and new violent truths.
I move silently through the rooms of my house,
if I make a mistake
the children will come to me at a
gallop and my affair with the rain
will stop.

The clock shows me its hand again
and the rain is still raining.
I close my eyes and make another wish:
you and I sitting on the rocks of
El Yeco, late at night or early
morning, waiting always for the light,
waiting for the good things the rain will bring
back to us. You extend your hand and say:
Look! Make a wish. There's a rainbow.
And in a single movement we braid our
hands and dream, both at the same time,
so we can keep it secret, and holy,
until death parts us.

Child's Eyes

People say that children see and hear things
they themselves cannot see or hear,
and this child breaking into
the room to hug and kiss
his grandmother, Wilma,
hasn't seen me yet.
I am afraid of his eyes,
touching like a hummingbird
the cornea of my eyes.
I don't want him to see
the puddle of
old pain and rusty love
that grows inside me,
the spider web of my disappointment,
a beaten heart that
has never overcome the loss of him.
I am afraid of this child
running around with his two frank
years, afraid of me breaking.
I'm sure he would scream
if I let my pupils touch his,
and the room would look
at me knowing the truth of
what he sees.
I am afraid and old,
smashing day after day
a memory of innocence.
I know too much.
My mind is futile.

Heartland

I wish I could put my heart
under the faucet in the sink
and with the running water
wash away the thumping
thoughts you evoke.

Who would guess that day I
saw you walking through the
long corridor in that estranged country
that you would stay in my mind until this day,
when there is not more of you
than these memories.

Thoughts of washing away
nostalgias and melancholies
jump into my brain,
as if water can
cure all our pains.

What can be more tragic than to die young?
The death of someone younger, maybe,
or the indifference of a people to such deaths.

How can we continue this way
to meet our gods if
our loved ones left us before?
Little consolation in knowing
there is no escape from death,
and as you sleep in your grave,
I will join you someday.

It is not the regret of not having been
able to love you more or deeper, or not
having said the unsaid, it is not
the regret of not having been better to you or
the others that I loved.

It is the certainty
that nothing can conquer
death and its humiliation
that bothers me today.

Red Robin

For Robin Gandy

*The numberless heart of the wind
beating above our loving silence.*

Pablo Neruda

How is it that after so many years
people are still talking about you?

Their envy
pulsates in their throats and temples,
creeps into their days,
scratches with long nails
their hearts and minds.

The first time I heard your laugh
I jumped, surprised.
It reminded me of the way
a beggar laughs in children's tales:
smoky and loud.

The entire
room looked back to you
and became a subtle dance
around your fingers.

The mathematicians there,
an obscure Stoltenberg and
a forever unknown Palmgren,

could not figure out
how a man as rebellious
and provocative toward the establishment
could enter a room and be King.
Is science always concerned with killing our illusions?
They took the smoke of your
pipe as an insult. Swedish
men cannot smoke pipes.
It is too expensive.

You didn't know they talked behind your back.
I'm here to tell you
so you know what to do with them.

The party was proper,
just a single moment
of farewell to their decadence.
The food was tasty
and the wine, as always, ran.

My friend and I ended up
doing dishes while all of you
discussed numbers about which we didn't care.

After you left, their comments:
your affair with Turing
your failure to follow in his footsteps.
Their throats and temples pulsating again.
They didn't want anything else
than to be in your shoes.

Who really cares about them?
Who will be remembered of them and their

work or their love stories?
After his suicide Turing left
all his papers to you, his student.

They didn't understand pre-cosmic
catastrophes or greatness or success.

He got his cure for death
and you got more love than you could handle.

Turing's heart was certainly well placed.
It is bad luck you couldn't see that in time.

Selective Exposure

In Detroit it is easy to see pheasants walking the alleys,
or children running like a flock hunting a dog,
murals of Jesus, Martin Luther King, Bob Marley
or B.B. King on dirty walls,
pink, velvet sofas covered by bags full of garbage,
falling sheer to the streets.
Sometimes old garages are semi-fallen
as if the breath
of a snowstorm will take them away.
And what to say about those houses:
they are hauling ghosts from another time.
It is easy to see pheasants walk in slumberous yards
with steps that show no rush.
You can see blacks with their privileges revoked,
whites preposterous about their color
walking by, face to face sometimes,
unaware of one another.
Detroit with its churches and voodoo,
fearful of God and the blues,
fearful of the truth.
He comes, goes, and dies in the hands of
a mortifier of flesh and souls.
One day He decided to visit a man
who left his church.
With chants, beseeched words, and promises of a
new beginning, He declared a holy war:
Love the World, He said.
I can't! the man answered.
Yes, you do! He defies. Here is my
blessing!

Love the world, He repeated.
The young man walked back to his house
to find a pheasant there, the pink velvet sofa,
the garages,
the houses,
the landscape is an arsonist.
Inside, he awakens
to wear the barren heart
given to him
when he was born
two thousand years before.

Parade

Cities without
mountains
lives without
conscience
bodies without
desire
surround me.

The smell of the spring
is here
memories
of a childhood
of multicolor pansies
and hyacinths.

I feel happy for a second.

I walk the long corridor
until I touch
completely
the vision
of the green field of Chanco.

Here I see her,
her face in a duel with the sun.
I hear the music of a
summer parade.

I see my pink communion dress in her hands.

I do not know her smell.
Life has evolved.

Cities without
mountains
lives without
conscience
bodies without
desire
do not hurt
as much
as the cold heart
of my mother.

Amnesia

Sometimes one forgets that
there do exist other mouths.
Sometimes one forgets that
there exist other meanings,
eyes, hands, bodies, codes,
that there exist other days,
other times,
the love of others.

One remembers
there exists much that one
would not want to forget.

Slowly they begin:
mouths,
eyes,
bodies,
codes,
others' love,
to seep through the walls
with Lucifer's subtlety,

and then one tries
to forget.

Boys

A torturer does not redeem himself through suicide.
                                        But it does help.
                                        – Mario Benedetti

The boys from the neighborhood,
some of them, stay behind the mud and the rain.

I ask myself what has become of
Romero, Quezada, Coleman?
Did their bodies and souls
escape deterioration?

Did they go into the army
to do their duty as soldiers
of the fatherland, the ones
who protect us from hate and
foreign tyrants?

Did they climb like the General
by usurping through disloyalty,
lies, secret codes and money?

Did they have families and
continue living in the city
as if nothing had happened?

Or did they sell their modest houses,
move to another neighborhood
where no one knows anything about them?

There they will come in the evening
to wash the remnants of blood
from their fingers.

Will they look for their wives,
give them a kiss, touch them
with those same hands?

Will their daytime nightmares
be cast upon those who
know nothing of where they
come at the end of the night?

Will they return their heads,
smashed by the memories they left
in the cells, streets, apartments to a soft warm
pillow that washes away their sins?

What happened to the men
I knew and never saw again?

Did they turn themselves into
men hungry for justice or
did they leave little by little in silence?

Did they put on their clothes
in the morning without knowing
whether they would return in
the evening to their dear ones?

Did they learn to kill in clandestine training or
did they become more manly with the
passing of these hard times?

Did they love like those
pure boys I met on those evenings
when to play was our universe?

Valentine's Day in Detroit

The sounds of children playing in the snow,
a bunch of orange roses and a sign
BE MY VALENTINE.
on the round surface of this day.

Are these moments similar
to the ones we dreamt of?
We couldn't answer, we are not others.
We are the ones standing still,
almost faceless.

Here we are inventing words
on this hammock despite
the baby spit.

A house untied to the ground,
a laundry room of nostalgia,
a window clouded by
little sleep,
a coat of memories we remove
every February,
a simple grin and a Sanders chocolate box,
then, we grow to the light like sweet peas.

Cyanide Smile

It is a crime that violates no law.

I learned it well at home
with Grandmother.

She hid her smile to use against us.

So powerful, so invisible,
that sword.

She knew if she used it
in small doses
she would find us like lambs.

She knew its power on a small scale.

Even war is not so cruel.

House

Thirty: just in time

For José Miguel Cruz

The night before your call, I dreamt of the ocean:
cold, dangerous, deep, dark, blue at dusk and dawn.
Taking a big breath, I left my body in this building
in the North for the Southern Hemisphere.
I fell into the arms of aunts and sisters
preparing a Sunday table, bountiful with
corn pie, tomato salad, green beans
and onions with cilantro,
thousand-layer cake and port from the Santa Rita's vineyard.
I saw my nieces and nephews
laughing with pleasure that lasted centuries.
The sweet, bitter, sandy taste of an oyster with lemon
reminded me of a place I was willing to die for.
I felt as if I didn't have a destiny,
I thought effort was not enough,
as if their lives were in vain.
It is clear to me, fights like this
are all won long before they are fought.
Where exactly?
At a Sunday table?
On a dark empty road that hides subversion?
In the kindness we summon, stirring the lawlessness within ourselves?
Thanks for your call.

me convierte en ese Yo de siempre
y me subyugo como esclava
bajo su dominio
enamorada
per secula seculorum.

Poem without a number: house

In this house,
covered to the ceiling with my insomnia,
spilling the evil
of a complex journey,
I remember:
a barricade. A homemade bomb
made by my hands,
the image of my lover and
in my head a semi-automatic
as redemption.
I beg forgiveness of all of you.
The rain is too thin to stop the fire.
My legs and arms are heavy.
Behind me, Santiago blazes
and bullets whiz at the sight of who we were,
ancestral pain I cannot shake off.
His body disappears from the earth into the air.
A heart spattered in the streets follows me in my defeat.
I think about you and
my house on fire,
the vision of my father fallen to his knees
praying for a miracle while
the rain disappears
in front of me.

en la Isla Quiriquina
el sumbido de las caracolas
anterior a llegada de los soldados

New

Death in Argentina

Mauricio was found at the morgue
with the inscription of NN
hanging from his left toe.

The Lucky Strike we shared finally killed him.
It is ironic that after all the gigantic genius
didn't kill him with a tank or modern M-16,
but the toxins of an addiction.

We both shared the same smokes
on numerous occasions. More than once he told
me he wanted to share more than that and once
he wanted to know if I smoked in bed after
making love. I coughed in surprise
but I did give him an answer: sometimes I do,
I said to him, sometimes I drink water from the faucet.
I was simpler than the fantasy he had about me.

Maybe just poets can understand each other,
even bad poets have another language. It is like
the words are invented only for those who love them.
We went to the movies once: we saw *Jules et Jim* by François Truffaut.

The Psychiatrist

If I remember correctly, I could not cry
until the baby was born. They wanted to shoot him.
I understood why Manuel Fernandez wanted
me to stay at the hospital after the birth.
I never told him anything about the group.
I could not trust him. I had to be strong
for my child. I needed to go the pump room
and leave my milk. You are suffering a post
partum depression, he told me, before I shot him,
like the many other voices in my head.

Exiles

Chanco had endless rows of white houses made of adobe
with thick terracotta shingles.
Old eucalyptus trees, taller than fifty feet, formed a natural barrier
        between the Pacific Ocean and the village.
The people made a living producing wine and cheese.
As a child I ran through the eucalyptus forest to the ocean
in a race with my half sibling.
Small roads of red clay covered by generations of fallen leaves
made for a cushioned walk for our sandals and bare feet.
I always won all the races.
Then, on the ocean, there would be another race to get rid of our
        clothes and be the first to jump into the water.
My mother would open a basket filled with bread, hardboiled eggs,
        cheese, blackberries picked by our own hands
and soda, spreading an old yellow tablecloth out on the sand.

Meanwhile Clemente would cut the watermelon he carried
from the house to the beach.
In Santiago things were different.
The day of the Coup, Mr. Monzalves visited us.
He sat on a sofa in our living room beneath a print of Picasso's
        Guernica.
My grandfather occupied one of the loveseats.
Later I came to know that Mr. Monzalves worked for DINA
(National Department of Intelligence).
My grandfather did not talk about what Mr. Monzalves said,
but it was clear that he knew that my grandfather
was a sympathizer of Allende and that he had come to deliver a
        warning.

Just before I left Chile the last person I met from the Front
in Santiago was my commander.
His real code name was *Wolf*.
I told him I was planning to leave the country because I could
        not avoid the surveillance anymore and my good friend,
the lawyer Insunza, had arranged for me to go to Sweden or France.

The Swedes were fond of Latin America's cause of liberation,
he had said, and they had been receptive to Chileans
from the beginning of the Coup.
Sweden is too far, go to the South, I can't, my family lives there,
        I told him.
He wanted to schedule a last rendezvous before my leaving.
I explained that it was exhausting to get to him in my condition.
I already had my visa and a plane ticket.
Still, I finally agreed to meet, changing between different
subway lines, moving to a taxi and then to a bus to avoid being
        followed.
I risked everything so that Wolf could make one last effort
to get me to stay.
He never appeared. I had wanted, at least, to say goodbye.
I left for Sweden on October 24, 1985, five weeks after
my daughter's father died.
Spring was beginning in Chile, as winter was in Sweden.
It would prove to be the coldest winter in one hundred years
with a mean temperature of -27.2°C in Vittangi.

A Mother Thing

When I got "home" from the hospital
there was a bed and a baby bed beside it, and a letter
from my mother that was forwarded from the refugee camp.
In the letter my mother said that she had missed the bus
that would have brought her from the South of Chile to the airport
          to say goodbye.
Somebody told her that I was leaving.
She had read about J's death in the newspapers. More
than a thousand people came to his funeral and the riots
that followed were covered on national TV. Reuters smuggled
pictures out of the country and in the archives of The Agency
that I would read twenty years later it would say: ...the case of J's
may turn into another scandal similar to the case concerning
the death of the three "degollados". The last paragraph
of the letter said "I hope now when you are a mother yourself
you can understand your own mother a little bit better."
I couldn't answer her. Not because I didn't have anything
to say but it was so hard to say it.
I wish I could have written something to her at that time to bring
          us closer.
But I still couldn't think clearly. It would be a long time before
          I could.

Words

Fourteen years feels like a century.
Memories of the last flight still linger.
My heart is pumping fast. My hands are cold.
My stomach crinching in a nut. I fear not breathing.
The image of my mother trying to tie me to a chair.
Was she crazy? She must have been. I will never know.
The language is unspoken but so familiar. I know this language.
I know this language and its power and defeat.
I cannot love in this language. I will never love in this language.
No Latin can be spoken by this river.

Daphne and non-profits in the Western Hemisphere

Her code name then was Daphne.
She recruited me in September of 1983,
three months before the official launch of
the organization. No other
students were invited, not even the boyfriend. We were
forty-five members in the entire country when
we started and at least four hundred at its peak,
and seventy-five in the metropolitan area that
covered five million people. It was fun
to be with them at some moments.
I learned their code names and their laughs
– or no laughs – Francisca who laughs loud and smoky,
Wolf who laughs silently – attached to it.
We could not share much,
the tension was always too high.
The adrenaline addiction was the biggest problem
after two or three years of belonging,
cheap whiskey and wine rolled its own nightmare.

On Earth

It takes a few years to know the heart of a man
Grandmother whispered. Yelled, whispered:
we know his body first and then his words.

Among silences, we meander, lust
blinds our clarity, we meander.

The body as well words, so foolish a package.
Should we remain mute before speaking?

Hypocritical stillness, a heart sleeps in
the ground. We are doomed to repeat. We repeat.

Andres the Barbarian

He was a ghostly figure
walking in the house of my grandparents
with a pipe in his mouth and
the tobacco that smells like Gitanes
around him as if smoke were coming out of his hair.

He had a dark beard and anyone
who might see him in the streets could not
figure him out so easily. At moments he looked
like a type that could solve the problems of the world.

At other moments
he looked like a DINA,
a secret agent that
would beat the shit out of you
if he was in the mood.

My friend Cote was afraid of him.
She said he looked like a gangster, a mobster
with impeccable gray suits
and dark glasses covering his melancholic eyes.

He was for some an electrical
engineer hired
by a firm to electrify
buildings across the country.
I don't know which was the real him.

It changed everything for him
if I didn't spell Hermanos with the "H" in it.

I do remember some good times with him,
like when he came back from a trip to Easter Island and
Grandmother and I got a pink pearl necklace from the natives.

For me he was the man who taught me to read,
and the man who hit me in the head
every time I forgot the letter "H".
How can I pronounce the letter "H"
if it didn't have any sound?

He could not forgive the error, that simple detail.
The fact that he did belong to the National Party
didn't mean much to us.
Family is family. Grandfather loved his son.
The issue with the letter "H" was the worst.
I do remember his books lined up in alphabetical
order in his room.

Number 7

For the son I never had let these green tears
open some fuchsias.

His skin glistens when I bathe him,
read a lullaby before bed.

For the son I never had let lilacs bloom,
close eyes when sorrow never heals.

Let me cut some roses from my yard,
chanting this dark song tonight.

The middle of this goodbye

You returned by the bus that will drop us
at the San Camilo bakery.

There you and I will order
two Napoleons and two coffees.

We will sit at the table, you will look around
to check if everything is the same.

I will sit a bit away from you and look for a mirror
where I can find my reflection and fix my hair.

You will take out your shopping bag and ask me if I
like the blouse and the perfume.

I will eat a piece of Napoleon and I will complain.
I will remain quiet, trying to understand how it is possible

that my list can be so long when I am marking everything missing.
This time you will give me your list, full of incomprehensible
        requests:

go to Mass on Sundays, talk to the girls.
I will bring my chair closer.

God is

People were killed
far from kingdoms
in the river of blood
of the new Pedro Donoso.
Memories soar. Who would believe
now in the pleasant countryside
and the tasty grapes of our vineyards?
We were closer to death
and despair. Were we closer to God?

The tale of two uncles

I grew up seeing his pictures everywhere in the house.
After the coup d'état we hid his pictures in drawers
as you do with those uncles you need to hide
for whatever reason.
Everything changed. The most
profound and the most simple. I didn't
die, as I used to think, if I didn't live in
Santiago. The sun used
to rise between the mountains and the certainty
that when the sun was right behind
the tallest tip of the mountains facing the
city was the time to go to school. I didn't need
a watch to know the time. At evening when
I went back home a dusky red
entered my pupils and produced a fast pace to
my heart every time. Santiago was a dirty city
with pollution year round, full
of danger and poverty, excitement and wealth,
two small worlds for too many people.
Allende wanted to do something about it.
Sam looked at him severely.

Counting Stars

On a quiet summer's night
Elena surprised me by saying, "If you continue
bothering those stars, warts are going
to fill your hands."
I thought those things never happened.
I counted all those stars
one by one, and the next day
the first itching on my right hand began.

I counted up to fifty many years later,
and stopped. Bothering a dark blue sky
could cause problems.
I prayed to Saint Therese
not to punish me. Not to send me warts.
I'd look at the sky and keep quiet.

Cattys

I spoke with Cattys last night.
Six hours' difference
between the hemispheres.
Max, her youngest,
answered the phone:
"Hon ligger och sover,"
he said, in his cute Swedish accent.
"Go and wake her up,"
I exclaimed with my corrupted one.
We wondered about the two years
of silence and what was spoken last.
This time I had prepared myself
to speak with her, longer.
I listened to Swedish music
for three weeks. Old
songs by Roxette, Mikael
Wiehe, Lisa Ekdahl.
When I speak with Cattys
my face uses different muscles.
Her laugh a bouquet of wild
flowers we collected
in Uppsala in the summer
time. Our children
running and stepping
into the lake
leaving us with no
possibilities for a good tan.
Our husbands away
with their addictions –
smoking, riding horses,

at a blackboard writing algorithms...
When she comes to the
phone I find white *algodón* clouds
in a baby blue Swedish "himlen"
a smörgås with
Kalles kaviar and
cucumber slices.
But overall I sense
Cattys' strength –
the candle in the dark Uppsala winters,
the whisper of an uggla when we went to bed alone,
the tons of white heavy snow the day just before Christmas,
the sisterhood that
never disappears,
not even under the Scandinavian skies.

The year of the plague

And in that place where no one lives in,
rain and sun should step in. No one sleeps
in their beds, we are all in danger.
Love is disappearing into the sky,
into the darkness.

Your lovely blue eyes are only ashes.
And your lovely body full of secrets
is crushed. You see, my love,
how history has changed us?

He offered you his bowl of deafness
for my songs: the one who laughs
last always laughs loudest.
Your thief's kisses are sorrow,
and rain is spilling over the Black Forest.

At the end of the hour

We had to put your coffin
in the ground. I threw the first
red carnation inside the grave,
it was when the first teargas
grenade exploded. The two policemen
reached with their hands for their guns.
A second teargas grenade exploded
closer to your new hard bed.

I was a bride. In my dark dress
I did not want to run,
I closed my eyes and saw you walking
through the hall of the Faculty.
What a wonderful season!
Tulips smelled like tulips,
the sun was the sun.
The noises of the gas

tearing apart the air
of the pala with the soil hitting
the cover of your maroon coffin.
If your neighbor's grave said
"God is fulfilled" how can I
return if they kill people like us?
Earth betrayed us.

Hunger

For Bobby Sands

The news broke then:
1981. Bobby Sands and
nine others are dead.

We planned a short
protest in the streets.

Many will do as he did.
We can't stop the
strikes around the world.

In Detroit and
London others
died of heart attacks
provoked by obesity.
Here, nobody knows who
Bobby Sands is.

In Manistee

1. In this city,

they had gardens where the sun rose
face to face with the sand.
They had rainbows, like us,
thirsty and wild.
They had emptiness like us.
Every gesture they make,
a heart is born from their bodies,
and, surprised, disappears into the air.

2. In this city, on the roofs:

things glisten. The roof is higher
than the clouds. Near to the point of shutting
down the sky from persistent streets.
And you stand still: between the
aluminum where the sun fits like a drummer,
completing your life.
You are not there.
The city changes,
the city rolls headlines of tears from the roofs.

3. In this city: like pages of a telephone book:

the newspaper announced today the city
is cutting off all public telephones from the streets.

The city keeps us inside. It makes images blurry.
It settles in cold drops on telephone wires.

You go slowly on skis in winter sun,
through brush where a few leaves hang on.
They are like pages of a telephone book
with the names eaten by the cold.

In this city, it is beautiful
to hear the hearts pulsing,
but shadows are more real than our bodies.

4. In this city, questions:

with the sky open to so many
God is closer in distance,
is why the earth is so populated.

You have to be human
to be disturbed,
the animals we eat are disturbed.
We flow in between cows and
chickens, disturbed by the city:

women were killed with green
and pink ribbons in their hair.
Men without souls marching
from the past to sit where a fallen
angel sits.

5. In this city, so much effort

So much effort to be a dog,
dream in their vigil.
And daggers dominate,
what moon without stables what nudes
of flushed, indestructible flesh.
And on the trunk,
a boy strains to be a fierce saint,
while the saint remains
invisible, small with
no strains at all.

After Death

They opened the door,
she saw their faces
covered with white feathers.

The long honey hair
strewn, on the floor.
The long curls –

she saw the sea
algae along the coast
of the Pacific Ocean.

"I want to be someone
else, but keep my dress, I want my dress
my shoes and my pink underwear."

A flood of tears
fell through their eyes.
They tried to hide them.

They didn't say one
word as they finished shaving her
imperfect round head.

Chiloe Island

The room was small and cheap.
As darkness settled over the capital of Santiago,
a thin crucifix hung above the headboard.

A garden in the blanket's embroidery
embraced simple copihues and violets,
and when we glanced at these threads

they seemed to blink at us.
Who could have the time to embroider
tiny blue, yellow, red flowers

on the borders of this quilt?
An old woman who knew of the resilient
shape of a young woman's heart,

asleep for the first time with her husband?
No evil hand makes such a garden.
Still, we breathed a fear of torture

and when he came back to the hotel, after his
lens in photography class saw everything,
we ran up the street to a restaurant.

The smell of curantos and fresh bread
and corn pie was a reminder we could stay
there forever among shellfish

and fishermen with red cheeks,
knives in harsh hands that opened
that traitor Pacific Ocean.

How the ocean eats bodies in silence,
in an act of revenge, but succulent waters
spit up oysters or fish.

When we went back to the room,
he called me to warm his body.
We fell asleep as two old friends.

He made me promise if we ever had
a child, and if he was not there, I would leave the country.
I slept like a cat until morning

The noisy street opened long before my eyes,
and as I was going for my breakfast
everyone else was going for lunch.

He wanted me to pose with a lobster.
I agreed only if it was the last time
he made me touch shellfish.

Code Names

The adrenaline addiction was the biggest
problem after two or three years. I learned
their laughter before code names,
but sometimes it was the other way around.
Her name was Daphne. No other students
were invited. She recruited me in September
of 1983. I should have died but the devil
did not want me. We lost our taste for food.
We got used to each other's silence.
We became addicted to pills. Like that, we lived
half useless, but the other half drank cheap
whiskey to forget that some of us might die.
How everything changed for me in Chile.
The sun used to rise between the mountains,
but now it fought its way into pollution and darkness.
Nobody bothered to love anyone too long.

Notes

'Sunday Walk, Urban Talk'
O'Higgins Park: Public park in Santiago, Chile
Alhue Street: Name of the street where Ignacio Recaredo
Valenzuela was assassinated in what was called *Operación Albania* or
Corpus Christi.
Pedro Donoso: Third chapter of the *Operación Albania* or *Corpus
Christi* where 7 other bodies of members of the opposition to
Pinochet were found in 1987.

'The Rain'
El Yeco: A small beach located in the V region 380 km of Santiago
of Chile.

'Red Robin'
Robin Gandy: Student and lover of Alan Turing

'Parade'
Chanco: Small town in the south of Chile

'Exiles'
DINA: *Direccion Nacional de Inteligencia Chilena*/Directorate of
National Intelligence of Chile.

Acknowledgements

Some of these poems were originally published in the following journals:

Passages North: 'Death in Argentina'; 'The Psychiatrist'; *The Aldebaran Review*: 'Exiles'; 'A mother thing'; *Crack the Spine, Issue 47*: 'On Earth'; *The Bacon Review*: 'Andres the barbarian', 'The tale of two uncles', 'Daphne and non-profits in the Western hemisphere'; *2River*: 'Number 7'; *Tygerburning Literary Magazine*: 'God is'; *The Adroit Journal*: 'The middle of this goodbye'; *Working Words: Punching the Clock and Kicking Out the Jams (Coffee House Press)*: 'Boys'; *Editions d'Arts Le Sabord*: 'Cattys'; *New Issues Press*: Michigan Writers Anthology: 'In Manistee'; *Ghost Town Literary Magazine*: 'After Death', 'Code Names'; *The Acentos Review*: 'Chiloe Island'.

Infinite thanks to Todd Swift for bringing this book into the world.

Also by Mariela Griffor:
Exiliana (2007, Luna Publications, Toronto) Canada
House (2007, Mayapple Press, Bay City, Michigan) USA

EYEWEAR POETS

MORGAN HARLOW MIDWEST RITUAL BURNING
KATE NOAKES CAPE TOWN
RICHARD LAMBERT NIGHT JOURNEY
SIMON JARVIS EIGHTEEN POEMS
ELSPETH SMITH DANGEROUS CAKES
CALEB KLACES BOTTLED AIR
GEORGE ELLIOTT CLARKE ILLICIT SONNETS
HANS VAN DE WAARSENBURG THE PAST IS NEVER DEAD
DAVID SHOOK OUR OBSIDIAN TONGUES
BARBARA MARSH TO THE BONEYARD
MARIELA GRIFFOR THE PSYCHIATRIST
DON SHARE UNION
SHEILA HILLIER HOTEL MOONMILK